MY INNER VOICE
Daily Affirmations to
Master My Journey

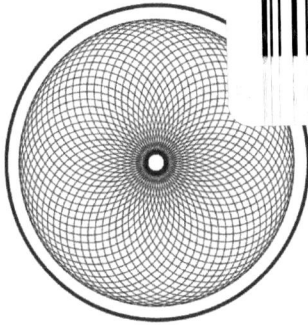

I0083007

365 Affirmations to Awaken
Your Inner Power

Chady Elias

My Inner Voice: Daily Affirmations to Master My Journey

365 Affirmations to Awaken Your Inner Power

This book is part of *In The Zone* Collection

Copyright © 2024 Chady Elias – Chady, LLC **All rights reserved.**

Cover Artwork © 2024 by Artist Chady Elias. All rights reserved. Cover Design by Chady Elias.

All rights reserved. Tous droits réservés.

No part of this publication may be reproduced or translated through any mechanical, photographic, electronic or phonographic process, stored in a retrieval system or transmitted in any form, without prior written permission from the copyright owner, except in the case of brief quotations embodied in articles or reviews. This book may not be reproduced in any form unless express permission is granted by the copyright owner. Unauthorized usage is prohibited.

For additional information contact ChadyElias.com

This Book is designed and intended for the individual, as a guide for self-help. No part of this book or any information contained within it constitutes professional treatment for any condition or clinical disorder, and is not considered an adequate substitute for professional or medical help. When distress in any form is experienced, one should seek professional guidance immediately.

ISBN 978-1-965668-03-0 (Paperback)

Chady LLC
Miami, FL
Printed 2025

To Ana Maria,
my love, my anchor,
my inspiration.

To Sophie and Zoie,
you are the light that
guides me forward.

This book carries my heart,
and my heart will always carry you.

~ Chady Elias

ABOUT THIS BOOK

Inside each of us, there is a voice.
Quiet, steady, true.
It is not the voice of fear, comparison, or doubt, it is the voice of knowing, purpose, and peace.

My Inner Voice is a collection of 365 daily affirmations to help you reconnect with that voice, the one that guides you toward your highest self. These words are here to realign you with your truth, remind you of your worth, and gently empower you to live each day from a place of clarity and intention.

This is not just a book of affirmations.
It is a sacred mirror. A daily practice. A return home.
Each affirmation is a spark to light your path, center your mind, and elevate your energy.

You can start on any day.
You can revisit the same affirmation as many times as your soul needs it.
You can read them silently, speak them aloud, or write them in your journal.

What matters is that you listen... not just to the words, but to how they resonate within you.

This is your journey.
These are your reminders.
And your inner voice is ready to rise.

WHAT ARE AFFIRMATIONS

Affirmations are positive statements you say in the present tense to help change the way you think and feel. They help you focus less on negative thoughts and more on possibilities and inner strength. When you repeat affirmations often, especially with feeling and focus, your brain starts to build new patterns and connections. This process is called neuroplasticity, which means your brain can grow and change based on what you practice.

Scientifically, affirmations affect something in your brain called the reticular activating system, or RAS. This part of your brain acts like a filter, helping you notice what matters most to you. If you keep saying something like "I am confident," your brain starts looking for signs that support that belief. Over time, this helps you think, feel, and act in ways that match what you keep affirming.

Positive Affirmations can also help you feel less stressed. When you use them regularly, they activate areas of the brain that are linked to feeling good and knowing your worth. Scientists have seen this in brain scans, especially in a part of the brain called the ventromedial prefrontal cortex. Using affirmations can lower stress hormones like cortisol and make it easier for you to handle pressure or criticism.

To get the most out of affirmations, say them every day in a quiet and relaxed moment. You can say them out loud, write them in a journal, or even repeat them in your mind. What really matters is that you believe in what you're saying and feel the meaning behind the words. Affirmations aren't about pretending everything is perfect. They are about reminding yourself of your strength, even when things are hard.

SYMBOL MEANING

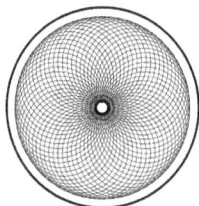

This symbol combines two sacred geometric forms: The Source and The Torus.

The large circle with the center circle represents The Source, symbolizing the origin and center of all things, with the central white dot signifying the core or focal point of this source.

This aspect of the symbol is also a representation of being "In The Zone," a state of flow where Spirit, Heart, Body, Mind are fully aligned, focused and in harmony.

The Torus mesh surrounding the central dot and filling the circle creating its border; signifies the continuous movement of energy, both spiritual and physical, within this zone.

Torus energy flows in a dynamic, circular pattern, symbolizing the harmonious exchange and balance between the spiritual and physical realms.

This combination of these two forms encapsulates the idea of interconnectedness, with energy continuously circulating through the source, embodying a state of unity and perpetual motion.

The Torus is roadmap for personal growth, symbolizes the cyclical nature of life's journey; where progress is not linear, but involves constant expansion and contraction.

In this framework, moments of success and "flow" represent the outward expansion, where everything seems to align and growth feels effortless.

These periods are balanced by inward contractions, where challenges, setbacks, or periods of confusion arise. Rather than viewing these as failures, the Torus teaches us that these dips are essential phases of growth, allowing us to turn inward, reassess, and realign with our core potential.

The continuous flow of energy within the Torus shows that even in moments of struggle, our connection to our inner source; the wellspring of creativity, strength, and potential; remains intact. It's a reminder that the energy is still flowing, even when it feels obstructed.

By understanding and applying this, we can embrace challenging times as opportunities for deeper self-awareness and personal refinement.

The Torus encourages us to cultivate practices like mindfulness, meditation, and self-reflection, which help us navigate the contractions with grace and patience.

The Torus is more than a symbol; it's a guide for understanding that personal growth is a dynamic, ongoing process, where every phase is necessary and part of a larger pattern that leads us back to our true self, the source.

"I love and accept myself
unconditionally.

I am worthy of all the
wonderful things life offers.

I radiate love and positivity."

"I love the journey of personal growth.

Each day, I become a better version of myself.

I embrace change with open arms."

"I love my body and treat it
with respect.

I nourish it with healthy
choices and exercise.

I am grateful for its strength
and vitality."

"I love my mind and its
endless potential.

I am constantly learning and
evolving.

My curiosity and intelligence
guide me to new heights."

"I love the people in my life.

I am surrounded by
supportive and caring
individuals.

My relationships are filled
with mutual respect and joy."

"I love the work that I do.

My career brings me
fulfillment and purpose.

I contribute positively to my
field and make a difference."

"I love the beauty in everyday
moments.

I find joy in simple pleasures.

My life is rich with happiness
and contentment."

"I love the abundance that
surrounds me.

I attract prosperity and
wealth effortlessly.

My financial situation
improves every day."

Day 9

"I love the creativity that
flows through me.

I express my ideas freely and
with passion.

My creativity knows no
bounds."

"I love the peace and tranquility within me.

I cultivate calmness and serenity.

My inner world is a sanctuary of peace."

"I love the strength and resilience I possess.

I overcome challenges with grace and determination.

I am empowered by my own perseverance."

"I love the dreams I am pursuing.

My passions lead me to a fulfilling and joyful life.

I am dedicated to achieving my goals."

"I love the gratitude I feel for my blessings.

I appreciate everything I have.

My heart is full of thankfulness and joy."

"I love the positive impact I have on others.

I inspire and uplift those around me.

I am a beacon of light and hope."

"I love the life I am creating.

Every day, I take steps
towards my ideal future.

I am proud of the person I am
becoming."

"I am deserving of all the
happiness life has to offer.

I create my own joy and share
it with others.

I am a beacon of light and
positivity."

Day 17

"I am grateful for my journey
and the lessons I've learned.

Every experience has shaped
me into who I am today.

I honor my path and trust its
direction."

"I am in tune with my
intuition and inner wisdom.

I listen to my inner voice and
trust its guidance.

I make decisions with clarity
and confidence."

"I am living a life of purpose
and passion.

I follow my heart and pursue
my dreams.

I am fulfilled and happy in all
that I do."

"I know I am resilient and strong.

Challenges are stepping stones to my success.

I overcome obstacles with grace."

"I know I am worthy of
abundance.

Prosperity is my birthright.

I attract wealth and
opportunities effortlessly."

"I know I am surrounded by
love and support.

My relationships are
nurturing and uplifting.

I give and receive love freely."

"I know I am in control of my destiny.

My choices shape my future.

I make decisions that align with my highest good."

"I know I am constantly
growing and evolving.

Every day brings new
possibilities.

I embrace change with an
open heart."

"I know I am a powerful creator of my reality.

My thoughts and actions manifest my dreams.

I focus on what I want to attract."

"I know I am deserving of
success.

My hard work and dedication
pay off.

I celebrate my achievements
and strive for more."

"I know I am at peace with my past.

I release what no longer serves me.

I look forward to a bright and promising future."

"I know I am capable of making a difference.

My actions positively impact the world.

I am a force for good and change."

"I know I am in harmony with
the universe.

Everything unfolds perfectly
for me.

I trust the process and my
journey."

"I know I am filled with creativity and inspiration.

My ideas are valuable and unique.

I express myself with confidence and joy."

"I know I am deserving of self-love and care.

I prioritize my well-being.

I nurture my mind, body, and spirit."

"I know I am aligned with my purpose.

My passions guide me towards fulfillment.

I live a meaningful and purposeful life."

"I feel confident in my
abilities.

My self-belief attracts
success.

I am empowered to achieve
my dreams."

"I feel deserving of love and happiness.

Joy flows through me effortlessly.

I attract positivity and warmth."

"I feel resilient and strong.

I can handle any challenge
that comes my way.

Each obstacle is an
opportunity for growth."

"I feel abundant and prosperous.

Wealth flows to me from various sources.

I am open to receiving all the good life has to offer."

"I feel surrounded by supportive and loving people.

My relationships uplift and inspire me.

I give and receive love freely."

"I feel in control of my life.

My choices create my reality.

I am focused and determined
to reach my goals."

"I feel grateful for my
continuous growth.

Every day brings new
opportunities for learning.

I embrace change with
enthusiasm."

"I feel like a powerful creator of my destiny.

My thoughts and actions shape my future.

I manifest my desires with ease."

"I feel worthy of achieving great success.

My hard work and dedication lead to incredible results.

I celebrate my accomplishments with pride."

"I feel at peace with my past
and excited for my future.

I release what no longer
serves me.

I embrace the present
moment with joy."

"I feel like a positive influence in the world.

My actions inspire and uplift others.

I am making a meaningful impact."

"I feel in harmony with the universe.

Everything is unfolding perfectly for me.

I trust the journey and the process."

"I feel creative and inspired.

My ideas flow effortlessly.

I express myself with
confidence and joy."

"I feel deserving of self-care
and love.

I prioritize my well-being.

I nurture my mind, body, and
spirit."

"I feel aligned with my true purpose.

My passions guide me towards fulfillment.

I live a life of meaning and intention."

"I see my potential clearly.
Every day,

I move closer to my goals.

I am capable of achieving
greatness."

Day 49

"I see the abundance around me.

Opportunities for success are everywhere.

I attract prosperity into my life."

"I see love in every aspect of my life.

My relationships are filled with joy and harmony.

I am surrounded by supportive and caring people."

"I see the strength within me.

Challenges are opportunities to grow.

I am resilient and capable of overcoming anything."

"I see the beauty in every moment.

I am grateful for the present.

I cherish the little things that bring me joy."

"I see my path to success
clearly.

I am focused and determined.

Every step I take brings me
closer to my dreams."

"I see positivity in every situation.

My mindset attracts good things.

I choose to focus on the bright side of life."

"I see my creativity flourishing.

My ideas are valuable and unique.

I express myself with confidence and enthusiasm."

"I see my health improving
every day.

I take care of my body and
mind.

I am strong, vibrant, and full
of energy."

"I see the impact I make on the world.

My actions inspire others.

I am a force for good and positive change."

"I see the lessons in my experiences.

Every moment is an opportunity to learn.

I grow and evolve with each passing day."

"I see my worth clearly.

I am deserving of all the good things life has to offer.

I believe in myself and my abilities."

"I see harmony in my
surroundings.

My environment is peaceful
and uplifting.

I create a space that nurtures
my soul."

"I see the progress I am making.

Every small step counts.

I celebrate my achievements and look forward to new milestones."

"I see my future filled with
possibilities.

I am open to new experiences
and opportunities.

I trust that great things are
coming my way."

"I speak words of positivity
and encouragement.

My voice uplifts and inspires
others.

I create a ripple effect of
kindness and hope."

"I speak my truth with confidence and clarity.

My opinions and ideas are valuable.

I express myself authentically and fearlessly."

"I speak love into my
relationships.

My words nurture and
strengthen my connections.

I build a foundation of trust
and understanding."

"I speak success into my life.

My affirmations attract
abundance and prosperity.

I am aligned with the energy
of achievement."

"I speak gratitude for all that I have.

My heart is full of appreciation.

I recognize the beauty and blessings in my life."

"I speak resilience and
strength.

I am capable of overcoming
any challenge.

My words empower me to
rise above adversity."

"I speak peace into my mind
and heart.

I create a calm and serene
inner world.

My thoughts and words
promote tranquility."

"I speak health and wellness over my body.

I am vibrant, strong, and full of energy.

My body responds to my positive affirmations."

"I speak growth and progress.

I am constantly evolving and improving.

My words reflect my commitment to personal development."

"I speak creativity and
inspiration.

My ideas flow freely and
abundantly.

I share my unique gifts with
the world."

"I speak kindness and
compassion.

My words heal and comfort.

I spread love and
understanding wherever I go."

"I speak confidence and self-belief.

I trust in my abilities and potential.

My affirmations reinforce my inner strength."

"I speak joy and happiness.

I choose to focus on what brings me joy.

My words create a positive and uplifting reality."

"I speak faith and trust in the journey.

I believe everything is unfolding perfectly for me.

My words reflect my trust in the process."

"I speak abundance and prosperity.

I am open to receiving all the good that life has to offer.

My words attract wealth and success."

"I understand my worth and value.

I am deserving of love, success, and happiness.

I honor and respect myself fully."

"I understand that challenges are opportunities for growth.

Every obstacle is a chance to become stronger.

I embrace difficulties with a positive mindset."

"I understand the power of
my thoughts.

My mindset shapes my
reality.

I choose to think positively
and create a life I love."

"I understand that patience is key.

Great things take time.

I trust in the process and remain steadfast on my journey."

"I understand the importance
of self-care.

I prioritize my well-being.

I nurture my mind, body, and
soul every day."

"I understand that I am in
control of my happiness.

I create joy from within.

I choose to focus on what
makes me feel good."

"I understand that every day
is a new beginning.

I have the power to start
fresh.

I approach each day with
hope and excitement."

"I understand that I am a
work in progress.

Personal growth is a lifelong
journey.

I am proud of how far I have
come and excited for what's
ahead."

"I understand the value of
gratitude.

Being thankful attracts more
blessings.

I appreciate all the good in
my life."

"I understand that my
actions impact others.

I choose to act with kindness
and compassion.

I make a positive difference in
the world."

"I understand that I am
unique and special.

My individuality is my
strength.

I embrace and celebrate my
uniqueness."

Day 89

"I understand that success comes from perseverance.

I stay committed to my goals.

My determination leads me to victory."

"I understand the importance
of living in the present.

I let go of the past and don't
worry about the future.

I fully experience and enjoy
each moment."

"I understand that my
journey is my own.

I don't compare myself to
others.

I honor my path and trust its
timing."

"I understand the significance
of love and connection.

Building relationships
enriches my life.

I cultivate bonds that uplift
and inspire me."

"I am confident in my abilities.

I trust myself to make the right decisions.

Every step I take leads me closer to my goals."

"I am deserving of love and happiness.

I attract positivity and joy into my life.

My heart is open to receive all the good that comes my way."

"I am resilient and strong.

Challenges are opportunities
for growth.

I overcome obstacles with
grace and determination."

"I am worthy of success and
abundance.

Prosperity flows to me
effortlessly.

I embrace the wealth of
opportunities around me."

"I am surrounded by supportive and loving people.

My relationships are nurturing and fulfilling.

I give and receive love freely."

"I am in control of my
thoughts and emotions.

I choose to focus on the
positive.

My mindset creates a joyful
and peaceful life."

"I am constantly growing and
evolving.

Every day, I become a better
version of myself.

I embrace change and
welcome new experiences."

"I am a powerful creator of my reality.

My thoughts and actions shape my future.

I manifest my dreams with ease."

"I am at peace with my past and excited for my future.

I release what no longer serves me.

I live fully in the present moment."

"I am confident in my unique
talents and skills.

I have valuable contributions
to make.

I express myself authentically
and fearlessly."

"I am grateful for all that I have.

My heart is filled with appreciation.

I recognize and celebrate my blessings."

"I am healthy, strong, and full of energy.

I take care of my body and mind.

I prioritize my well-being every day."

"I am a beacon of positivity and inspiration.

My presence uplifts those around me.

I spread love and kindness wherever I go."

"I am worthy of self-love and care.

I treat myself with kindness and respect.

I nurture my mind, body, and spirit."

"I am aligned with my
purpose and passion.

I follow my heart and pursue
my dreams.

I live a life of meaning and
fulfillment."

"I do believe in my abilities.

I trust myself to achieve greatness.

Every action I take brings me closer to my goals."

"I do prioritize my well-being.

I nurture my mind, body, and spirit.

Self-care is a top priority in my life."

"I do embrace challenges as
opportunities for growth.

I face obstacles with courage
and resilience.

Every setback is a setup for a
comeback."

"I do attract abundance and
prosperity.

I am open to receiving all the
good life has to offer.

Wealth flows to me
effortlessly."

"I do cultivate loving and supportive relationships.

I surround myself with positive people.

My connections are meaningful and fulfilling."

"I do focus on the positive.

My thoughts create my
reality.

I choose to see the good in
every situation."

"I do commit to my personal growth.

I am constantly learning and evolving.

Every day, I strive to be the best version of myself."

"I do take inspired action
towards my dreams.

My efforts are aligned with
my goals.

I move forward with
confidence and purpose."

"I do live in the present
moment.

I let go of the past and don't
worry about the future.

I fully experience and enjoy
each day."

"I do express my creativity
freely.

My ideas are valuable and
unique.

I share my gifts with the
world."

"I do practice gratitude daily.

I appreciate all the blessings
in my life.

My heart is filled with
thankfulness."

"I do maintain a healthy and
balanced lifestyle.

I eat well, exercise, and rest.

My body is strong and full of
energy."

"I do spread positivity and kindness.

My words and actions uplift others.

I make a positive impact on the world."

"I do honor and respect
myself.

I set healthy boundaries and
prioritize self-love.

I am worthy of care and
compassion."

"I do pursue my passions
with enthusiasm.

I am aligned with my
purpose.

My life is filled with meaning
and fulfillment."

"I love and accept myself
unconditionally.

I am worthy of all the
wonderful things life offers.

I radiate love and positivity
to others."

"I love the journey of personal
growth.

Each challenge strengthens
my resilience.

I embrace opportunities to
learn and evolve."

"I love my body and treat it
with respect.

I nourish it with healthy
choices.

I am grateful for its strength
and vitality."

"I love my creative spirit and
nurture it daily.

My ideas flow effortlessly and
inspire others.

I am a conduit for creativity."

"I love the relationships in my life.

I cherish the bonds with family and friends.

I cultivate connections based on mutual respect and support."

"I love the work I do.

It brings me fulfillment and joy.

I contribute positively to my work environment and make a difference."

"I love the peaceful moments
I create for myself.

I prioritize self-care and
relaxation.

I am at ease and content in
my own company."

"I love the abundance that surrounds me.

I attract prosperity with my positive mindset.

Money flows to me easily and freely."

"I love the person I am
becoming.

I am growing into my best
self.

Each day, I am more
confident and empowered."

"I love the opportunities life presents to me.

I embrace change and new experiences.

I trust that everything happens for my highest good."

"I love the joy and laughter I bring into my life.

I find humor in everyday situations.

I am a source of positivity and happiness."

"I love the clarity and peace I
find in meditation.

I connect with my inner
wisdom and intuition.

I am centered and balanced."

"I love the dreams I am pursuing.

I am passionate about my goals.

I take consistent action towards making my dreams a reality."

"I love the impact I have on others.

I inspire and uplift those around me.

I am a catalyst for positive change in the world."

"I love the abundance of love
in my life.

I am surrounded by love and
warmth.

I give and receive love freely
and unconditionally."

"I speak words of
encouragement and
positivity.

My voice uplifts and inspires
those around me.

I am a source of motivation
and empowerment."

"I speak my truth with clarity
and confidence.

I express myself authentically
in all situations.

My words have power and
impact."

"I speak love and kindness
into every interaction.

My words create harmony
and understanding.

I cultivate meaningful
connections with others."

"I speak success into my life.

I am confident in my abilities
to achieve my goals.

I attract opportunities that
align with my highest good."

"I speak gratitude for all the blessings in my life.

I appreciate the abundance that surrounds me.

I attract more blessings by expressing gratitude."

"I speak resilience and strength into my challenges.

I face obstacles with courage and determination.

I am capable of overcoming any adversity."

"I speak health and vitality
into my body.

I nurture my well-being with
healthy choices.

I am strong, vibrant, and full
of energy."

"I speak creativity and inspiration into my endeavors.

My ideas flow freely and creatively.

I am a channel for innovative solutions and new perspectives."

"I speak confidence and self-belief into my journey.

I trust in my abilities and embrace my potential.

I am worthy of success and achievement."

"I speak peace and calmness
into my mind.

I release stress and worry
with each breath.

I am centered, grounded, and
at peace."

"I speak kindness and compassion to myself and others.

I treat myself with love and respect.

I spread kindness wherever I go."

"I speak abundance and prosperity into my life.

I am open to receiving all the wealth and opportunities the universe offers.

Money flows to me easily and effortlessly."

"I speak joy and happiness
into my experiences.

I choose to focus on the
positive aspects of life.

I am a magnet for joy and
laughter."

"I speak wisdom and intuition
into my decisions.

I trust my inner guidance to
lead me in the right direction.

I make choices that align with
my highest purpose."

"I speak transformation and growth into my journey.

I embrace change as an opportunity for personal development.

I am evolving into the best version of myself."

"I see opportunities for growth in every challenge.

I am resilient and capable of overcoming obstacles.

Each setback strengthens my determination."

"I see abundance flowing into
my life.

I attract prosperity and
wealth effortlessly.

The universe provides me
with everything I need."

"I see beauty and positivity in every situation.

I choose to focus on the good.

My optimistic outlook attracts positive outcomes."

"I see love and compassion in every interaction.

I am surrounded by supportive and caring individuals.

I give and receive love unconditionally."

"I see success in my future.

I am confident in my abilities
to achieve my goals.

Every step I take brings me
closer to my dreams."

"I see strength and resilience within myself.

I am capable of handling any challenge that comes my way.

I am empowered to take on new opportunities."

"I see clarity and purpose in my life.

I am aligned with my true calling.

My path is clear, and I walk it with confidence."

"I see health and vitality in my body.

I nourish myself with nutritious food and exercise.

I am strong, energetic, and in optimal health."

"I see creativity and inspiration flowing through me.

I am a vessel for innovative ideas.

My creativity enriches my life and those around me."

"I see gratitude and appreciation in my heart.

I am thankful for the abundance in my life.

I attract more blessings by expressing gratitude daily."

"I see harmony and balance in my relationships.

I cultivate meaningful connections with others.

I communicate openly and authentically."

"I see wisdom and clarity in my decisions.

I trust my intuition to guide me.

I make choices that align with my values and goals."

"I see joy and laughter in my daily experiences.

I find humor in life's challenges.

I embrace each moment with a positive attitude."

"I see opportunities for learning and growth everywhere.

I embrace change as a catalyst for personal development.

I am evolving into the best version of myself."

Day 167

"I see peace and serenity
within myself.

I release stress and negativity
with ease.

I am centered, grounded, and
at peace with who I am."

"I understand that I am
worthy of love and respect.

I attract positive and loving
relationships into my life.

I deserve happiness and
fulfillment."

"I understand that challenges
are opportunities for growth.

I embrace obstacles as
stepping stones to success.

I am resilient and capable of
overcoming anything."

"I understand the power of
my thoughts and beliefs.

I choose to focus on
positivity and abundance.

I attract prosperity and
success with my positive
mindset."

"I understand the importance of self-care and prioritize my well-being.

I nourish my body, mind, and soul with love and kindness.

I am deserving of care and rejuvenation."

"I understand that each day
is a new beginning.

I release the past and
embrace the present moment.

I create a future filled with
possibilities and
opportunities."

"I understand the value of forgiveness and compassion.

I forgive myself and others with ease.

I release resentment and embrace peace and healing."

"I understand that I am in control of my reactions and emotions.

I choose to respond with calm and positivity.

I create a peaceful and harmonious environment."

"I understand the importance of setting goals and taking action.

I set clear intentions and work towards them diligently.

I am committed to achieving my dreams."

"I understand that life is a journey of learning and growth.

I embrace new experiences and challenges.

I evolve into a stronger and wiser version of myself."

"I understand the power of gratitude.

I appreciate the blessings in my life.

I attract more abundance and joy by practicing gratitude daily."

"I understand that my beliefs shape my reality.

I believe in my potential and abilities.

I am capable of achieving greatness in all areas of my life."

"I understand the significance of patience and trust in the process.

I allow things to unfold naturally.

I trust that everything happens at the right time for my highest good."

"I understand that I am responsible for my own happiness.

I choose joy and positivity in every situation.

I radiate happiness and attract positive experiences."

"I understand the importance
of self-expression and
authenticity.

I honor my true self and
express myself freely.

I embrace my uniqueness and
celebrate my individuality."

"I understand that I am
constantly evolving and
growing.

I embrace change and
welcome new opportunities.

I am open to learning and
expanding my horizons."

"I am confident in my abilities
and talents.

I trust myself to handle any
challenge that comes my way.

I attract success with my
positive mindset."

"I am worthy of love and
respect.

I deserve to be treated with
kindness and compassion.

I attract loving and fulfilling
relationships into my life."

"I am resilient and strong.

I bounce back from setbacks with grace and determination.

I grow stronger with every obstacle I overcome."

"I am grateful for the abundance in my life.

I attract prosperity and wealth effortlessly.

Money flows to me from expected and unexpected sources."

"I am surrounded by supportive and encouraging people.

My relationships are nurturing and inspiring.

I give and receive love unconditionally."

"I am in control of my
thoughts and emotions.

I choose to focus on
positivity and optimism.

I create a joyful and peaceful
life for myself."

"I am constantly evolving and improving.

I embrace change as an opportunity for growth.

I am becoming the best version of myself every day."

"I am a magnet for success
and achievement.

I set clear goals and work
diligently towards them.

I celebrate my
accomplishments and
milestones."

"I am at peace with my past.

I release all resentment and forgive myself and others.

I live in the present moment with gratitude and acceptance."

"I am worthy of self-care and
self-love.

I prioritize my well-being and
nourish my body, mind, and
soul.

I am deserving of rest and
rejuvenation."

"I am a positive influence on others.

My words and actions inspire and uplift those around me.

I make a meaningful difference in the world."

"I am aligned with my
purpose and passion.

I follow my heart and pursue
my dreams fearlessly.

I live a life of purpose and
fulfillment."

"I am open to new opportunities and experiences.

I welcome change and embrace new challenges.

I trust that everything happens for my highest good."

"I am creative and innovative.

I tap into my creativity and
express myself freely.

My ideas are unique and
valuable contributions to the
world."

"I am worthy of happiness
and joy.

I choose happiness in every
moment.

I attract positivity and
abundance into my life."

"I feel confident and capable
in everything I do.

My self-belief empowers me
to achieve my goals.

I radiate positivity and
attract success."

"I feel grateful for the abundance in my life.

I appreciate all the blessings that come my way.

I attract more positivity with my thankful heart."

"I feel strong and resilient.

Challenges make me stronger
and wiser.

I embrace obstacles as
opportunities for growth."

"I feel deserving of love and happiness.

I attract loving and supportive relationships.

My heart is open to giving and receiving love."

"I feel at peace with myself
and the world around me.

I release all negativity and
embrace serenity.

I am centered and calm."

"I feel healthy and vibrant.

I nourish my body with nutritious food and exercise.

I am full of energy and vitality."

"I feel inspired and creative.

Ideas flow to me effortlessly.

I express my creativity with passion and joy."

"I feel connected to my inner wisdom.

I trust my intuition to guide me.

I make decisions confidently and purposefully."

"I feel grateful for my journey
of personal growth.

I embrace change and
welcome new experiences.

I am evolving into my best
self."

"I feel supported by the universe.

I trust in divine timing.

Everything unfolds perfectly for me."

"I feel motivated and determined.

I set clear goals and work towards them diligently.

I am committed to my success."

"I feel joyful and optimistic.

I choose happiness in every moment.

I attract positivity and good vibes."

"I feel worthy of all the good
things life has to offer.

I attract abundance and
prosperity effortlessly.

I am open to receiving
blessings."

"I feel like a positive influence on others.

My presence inspires and uplifts those around me.

I make a positive impact in the world."

"I feel aligned with my purpose.

I follow my passions with dedication and enthusiasm.

I live a meaningful and fulfilling life."

"I do embrace each day with optimism and joy.

I choose positivity in every situation.

My optimistic outlook attracts good things."

"I do believe in my ability to achieve my goals.

I am capable and determined.

Every step I take brings me closer to success."

"I do take care of my body, mind, and spirit.

I prioritize self-care and well-being.

I am strong, healthy, and full of energy."

"I do attract abundance into
my life.

I am open to receiving
prosperity.

Money flows to me
effortlessly and abundantly."

"I do nurture loving
relationships.

I am surrounded by
supportive and caring people.

I give and receive love
unconditionally."

"I do face challenges with courage and resilience.

Each obstacle is an opportunity for growth.

I overcome challenges with grace."

"I do celebrate my
achievements, big and small.

I acknowledge my progress
and successes.

I am proud of my
accomplishments."

"I do forgive myself and others easily.

I release resentment and negativity.

I choose peace and compassion in all situations."

Day 221

"I do attract positive
opportunities into my life.

I am open to new experiences
and adventures.

I welcome change with
enthusiasm."

"I do trust in the process of
life.

I surrender to divine timing.

Everything unfolds perfectly
for my highest good."

"I do express gratitude for all
that I have.

I appreciate the blessings in
my life.

Gratitude attracts more
abundance and joy."

"I do radiate confidence and positivity.

I believe in myself and my abilities.

I am worthy of success and happiness."

"I do inspire and uplift others.

My words and actions make a
positive impact.

I am a source of
encouragement and support."

"I do live with purpose and intention.

I follow my passions and dreams.

I create a meaningful and fulfilling life."

"I do cultivate inner peace
and serenity.

I am centered and balanced.

I embrace each moment with
mindfulness and gratitude."

"I am confident in my abilities
and attract success
effortlessly.

My hard work pays off and
leads to incredible
opportunities.

Every day, I am becoming
more prosperous and
fulfilled."

"I am a magnet for positivity
and growth.

My dedication opens doors
to endless possibilities.

I am aligned with abundance
and success in all my
endeavors."

"I radiate confidence and attract the right people and opportunities.

My passion and perseverance lead me to greatness.

I am worthy of all the success coming my way."

"I am capable of achieving anything I set my mind to.

Every challenge is an opportunity for growth.

I embrace my potential with confidence."

"I am deserving of love,
happiness, and success.

My positive attitude attracts
wonderful experiences.

I am grateful for all the
blessings in my life."

"I am a powerful creator of my reality.

My thoughts and actions shape my future.

I choose to focus on what brings me joy and fulfillment."

"I am resilient and can overcome any obstacle.

Each setback is a setup for a comeback.

I trust in my ability to find solutions and thrive."

"I am surrounded by supportive and loving people.

My relationships bring me joy and strength.

I give and receive love freely and abundantly."

"I am constantly growing and evolving.

Each day, I become a better version of myself.

I embrace change and see it as a path to success."

"I am worthy of all the good things life has to offer.

My self-worth is not determined by external validation.

I believe in myself and my dreams."

"I am in control of my
thoughts and emotions.

I choose to focus on the
positive and let go of
negativity.

I create a peaceful and joyful
life."

"I am grateful for my body and its incredible abilities.

I nurture it with love and care.

I am healthy, strong, and full of energy."

"I am creative and my ideas
are valuable.

I express myself freely and
confidently.

My creativity brings joy and
inspiration to others."

Day 241

"I am open to new experiences
and opportunities.

I trust that life has amazing
adventures in store for me.

I embrace the unknown with
excitement."

"I am financially abundant
and attract wealth easily.

Money flows to me from
multiple sources.

I use my resources wisely and
generously."

"I am confident in who I am.

I trust my inner guidance.

I walk my path with strength and grace."

"I love and accept myself fully.

I honor my journey.

I radiate peace and authenticity."

"I feel joy in the present moment.

I let go of worry.

I embrace life with an open heart."

"I see abundance all around
me.

I attract prosperity easily.

I am open to receiving
blessings."

"I speak my truth with
courage.

I express myself freely.

I honor my voice and story."

"I do take care of my body and mind.

I nourish myself daily.

I am vibrant and full of life."

"I understand that I am enough.

I release comparison.

I celebrate my unique gifts."

"I am aligned with my purpose.

I follow my passions.

I live with meaning and direction."

"I love the person I am
becoming.

I grow with intention.

I embrace each step of my
evolution."

"I feel strong and capable.

I overcome challenges.

I rise with resilience and faith."

"I see beauty in everyday moments.

I cherish the now.

I create joy through presence."

"I speak love and kindness.

My words uplift.

I spread compassion wherever
I go."

"I do believe in my dreams.

I act with purpose.

I manifest success with clarity."

"I understand the power of gratitude.

I give thanks freely.

I attract more to be grateful for."

"I am a beacon of light.

I inspire others.

I share my energy with positivity."

"I love the peace within me.

I trust the stillness.

I find strength in calm."

"I feel supported by the universe.

I trust divine timing.

Everything unfolds perfectly for me."

"I see opportunity in every challenge.

I grow from experience.

I thrive through change."

"I speak confidence and faith.

I believe in my future.

I align with success."

"I do embrace my creativity.

I let ideas flow.

I express my gifts with joy."

"I understand that healing
takes time.

I am patient with myself.

I honor my process."

"I am worthy of happiness.

I invite joy in.

I choose positivity each day."

Day 265

"I love the life I am creating.

I build it with love.

I am proud of my path."

"I feel grounded and secure.

I trust my foundation.

I walk forward with ease."

"I see my growth clearly.

I celebrate my wins.

I move with purpose and hope."

"I speak truth with love.

I connect deeply.

I nurture honest
relationships."

"I do honor my needs.

I listen within.

I care for my heart and soul."

"I understand that life is a gift.

I live with wonder.

I savor each breath."

"I am resilient and adaptable.

I trust myself in change.

I grow through every season."

"I love how far I've come.

I celebrate progress.

I look ahead with excitement."

"I feel connected to all life.

I walk with compassion.

I contribute with love."

"I see peace in my future.

I build it now.

I let harmony lead the way."

"I speak with clarity and intention.

My words matter.

I share my message boldly."

"I do take inspired action.

I move with direction.

I co-create my dreams."

"I understand my value.

I honor my worth.

I stand tall in my truth."

"I am open to miracles.

I welcome the unexpected.

I trust the magic of life."

"I love the energy I radiate.

I am magnetic.

I draw beauty and joy to me."

"I feel worthy of love.

I give and receive freely.

My heart is open and whole."

"I see my inner light.

I shine brightly.

I uplift the world around me."

"I speak calm into my day.

I flow with ease.

I breathe peace into every moment."

"I do forgive myself.

I release the past.

I choose peace and healing now."

"I understand my emotions.

I welcome them with care.

I listen with empathy."

"I am full of potential.

I explore with courage.

I create a life I love."

"I love my body.

I respect its wisdom.

I treat it with care and love."

"I feel grateful for today.

I live in wonder.

I invite joy into every moment."

"I see success unfolding.

I take aligned steps.

I trust my unique journey."

"I speak life into my dreams.

I empower my vision.

I believe in my path."

"I do set healthy boundaries.

I protect my peace.

I honor my needs daily."

"I understand the power of
rest.

I give myself space.

I allow renewal and balance."

"I am in harmony with life.

I move with rhythm.

I flow with divine timing."

"I love the freedom within me.

I release limitation.

I soar with confidence."

"I feel the presence of love.

I am never alone.

I walk with grace and trust."

Day 295

"I see the lessons in all things.

I grow in wisdom.

I evolve through experience."

"I speak encouragement daily.

I cheer myself on.

I motivate my heart with kindness."

"I do make a difference.

My presence matters.

I am a force of light and impact."

"I understand my purpose.

I walk it fully.

I give my gifts to the world."

"I am courageous and bold.

I try new things.

I explore life fearlessly."

"I love who I am.

I honor every part.

I am whole, evolving, and
complete."

Day 301

"I feel harmony in my spirit.

I am aligned.

I live in joyful balance."

"I see myself with love.

I release judgment.

I embrace my humanity."

"I speak joy into my day.

I laugh freely.

I welcome delight and play."

"I do trust the unknown.

I move with faith.

I dance with life's mysteries."

"I understand that I belong.

I am accepted.

I am loved for who I am."

"I am focused and
determined.

I pursue my goals with
clarity.

I achieve what I set my heart
to."

"I love my ability to grow.

I learn from every experience.

I rise stronger each time."

"I feel inspired by life.

I notice the wonder around
me.

I allow creativity to guide
me."

"I see joy in small things.

I celebrate tiny victories.

I am present in each moment."

"I speak truth from the heart.

I communicate with kindness.

I build trust through honesty."

Day 311

"I do value my time.

I use it wisely.

I invest in what nourishes my soul."

"I understand that I am
evolving.

Change is a gift.

I embrace my
transformation."

"I am open to connection.

I attract meaningful
relationships.

I share love and
understanding."

"I love how life flows through me.

I am one with its rhythm.

I move with grace."

"I feel excited about my future.

I welcome the unknown.

I trust what's coming is beautiful."

"I see peace as my foundation.

I return to it often.

I anchor myself in calm."

"I speak vision into my days.

I plan with intention.

I live with purpose."

"I do trust myself completely.

I listen within.

I follow my heart with confidence."

"I understand that rest is
sacred.

I allow myself to pause.

I restore my inner world."

"I am magnetic to miracles.

I welcome blessings.

I open to the extraordinary."

Day 321

"I love my mind.

I think clearly and creatively.

I honor my intelligence."

"I feel empowered in my choices.

I shape my path.

I stand in my power."

"I see myself as a light.

I bring warmth and joy.

I illuminate the lives I touch."

"I speak with joy and sincerity.

My words are uplifting.

I inspire others through my voice.

"I do take bold steps forward.

I trust my direction.

I act with purpose and fire."

"I understand that love
begins with me.

I give to myself.

I radiate love outward."

"I am deeply rooted and open.

I stay grounded while growing.

I balance strength and flow."

"I love the adventure of life.

Each day is a gift.

I wake up with gratitude."

"I feel whole and complete.

I am enough.

I celebrate my presence."

"I see grace in every
experience.

I let life teach me.

I grow with acceptance."

"I speak peace in tense moments.

I stay calm and centered.

I choose softness over struggle."

"I do care for my emotions.

I give myself space to feel.

I process with kindness."

"I understand that my energy
is sacred.

I protect it.

I choose where I shine."

"I am excited to create today.

I am a vessel for beauty.

I express myself fearlessly."

"I love being alive.

I treasure this moment.

I breathe in possibility."

"I feel a divine presence within me.

I walk with faith.

I am supported always.

"I see my dreams unfolding.

Step by step, I arrive.

I trust the timing of my life."

"I speak with authenticity.

I let my truth be known.

I connect through honesty."

"I do appreciate where I am.

Every season has meaning.

I bloom in my own time."

"I understand that my worth
is unshakable.

I am valuable just as I am."

"I am constantly expanding.

My heart, mind, and soul grow.

I welcome evolution."

"I love my soul's journey.

It is sacred and true.

I walk it with reverence."

"I feel ease in my body.

I move with awareness.

I honor my physical being."

"I see magic in the mundane.

Beauty lives in simplicity.

I find joy in the ordinary."

"I speak with confidence and care.

I am heard and respected.

My words carry power."

"I do embrace my intuition.

It is wise and guiding.

I trust its gentle whispers."

"I understand that
boundaries are love.

I set them with clarity.

I protect my peace."

"I am a source of joy.

I spread laughter and light.

I make the world brighter."

"I love learning new things.

My curiosity is alive.

I grow with excitement and wonder."

"I feel calm even in chaos.

I center myself.

I return to my breath and presence."

"I see opportunity in every
moment.

Life supports me.

I act with faith and courage."

"I speak love into my day.

I choose kindness first.

I let compassion lead the way."

"I do move forward fearlessly.

I release hesitation.

I step into possibility."

"I understand the value of silence.

I find peace in stillness.

I listen to my soul."

"I am aligned with love.

I treat myself gently.

I allow my heart to open fully."

"I love waking up to a new
day.

It's a fresh start.

I begin with gratitude."

"I feel balanced and in flow.

I manage my energy well.

I respect my own rhythm."

"I see my inner power.

I access it with love.

I use it to lift others too."

"I speak my needs with clarity.

I am worthy of being heard.

I communicate with grace."

"I do believe in goodness.

I see it in myself and others.

I invite it in daily."

"I understand that patience
brings peace.

I wait with grace.

I trust the unfolding."

"I am the author of my story.

I write it with intention.

I create what I envision."

Day 363

"I love what I am becoming.

I honor my pace.

I trust the unfolding of me."

"I feel supported by life.

I am held and guided.

I rest in that truth."

Day 365

"I see my dreams as seeds.

I water them daily.

I trust they will bloom."

WHAT IS NEXT?

Master Your Journey

I invite you to join *Master Your Journey* - a transformative community designed to help you unlock your full potential, eliminate confusion, and create a life of fulfillment and success. This isn't just a group; it's a movement of like-minded individuals stepping into their highest selves.

In *Master Your Journey*, you'll gain access to cutting-edge tools, live coaching, and powerful courses designed to align your thoughts, actions, and energy with success.

With your own AI Virtual Coach; trained with my expertise; you'll receive tailored guidance every step of the way.

The time for transformation is NOW. No more waiting, no more "someday"; *your next level begins today.*

Scan this QR code to know more and to Start Your Free 7-Day Trial

MASTER YOUR JOURNEY

Books:

PUBLICATIONS

Explore my other books and workbooks that dive deeper into creativity, personal growth, and self-discovery. Scan the QR code to check them out.

Blogs:

I regularly write blogs that explore creativity, human experiences, and art. Join me in these thought-provoking discussions by reading my latest posts. Scan the QR code to start reading.

BLOG

Coaching:

COACHING

Explore and live the endless horizons of achievement. There are no boundaries to what one can achieve. Scan the QR code to start the conversation with me.

Speaking & Podcasting:

Scan this QR code to book me for speaking engagements and podcast interviews.

BOOK ME

ABOUT THE AUTHOR

Chady Elias is a visual artist, creativity coach, business strategist, hypnotherapist, and NLP practitioner based in Miami, Florida. With a Master's in Fine Arts and extensive experience in creativity, personal development, and transformational coaching, Chady helps individuals and businesses break creative barriers, align with their purpose, and achieve extraordinary growth.

Chady's work is rooted in the belief that self-awareness, innovation, and strategic transformation are the keys to reaching the next level; whether in art, business, or personal success. Through his artwork, coaching programs, corporate training, workshops, and writings, he empowers others to explore their inner world, redefine their vision, and create impactful change.

His personal journey is a testament to the power of belief, creativity, and limitless potential. By combining artistic expression, subconscious reprogramming, and business strategy, Chady has developed a unique methodology for unlocking human and entrepreneurial potential.

Know more about Chady

ABOUT CHADY ELIAS

www.ingramcontent.com/pod-product-compliance
Lightning Source LLC
Chambersburg PA
CBHW030909090426
42737CB00007B/142